A Day in India

Written and photographed
by Jonathan and Angela Scott

Contents

Collins

Where I live

My name's Gini and I live in Jaipur, India.
It's a big city and I love it.
There's always so much happening.

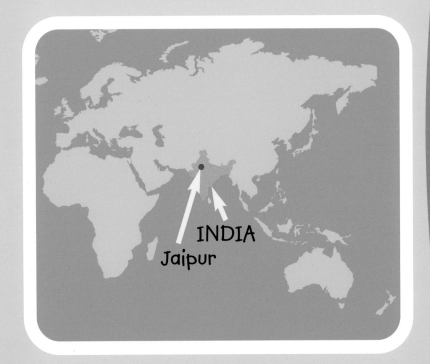

INDIA
Jaipur

Jaipur is a big and busy city.

My family

I've got a big family and we all live in the same house. There's my great granny and my aunts and my uncles and cousins as well as my mum, dad and little brother Raj. I think Raj gets away with a lot, because he's the youngest. I play with my cousin Nila every day.

my aunty

my brother Raj

Mum

my cousin

my cousin Nila

my great granny

me

Dad

4

Here I am with Nila.

In the morning

In the morning, Dad goes off first, because he starts work very early. Mum makes yoghurt for our breakfast, and then she sometimes goes to help Dad in his office. Nila and her brother go to a different school from me. That's because they're older.

It's busy at home when everyone's getting ready in the morning. Mum's making yoghurt and talking on her mobile to Dad at the same time.

Going to school

Sometimes we go through the market on the way to school. I love that because there's always so much to see, but we haven't got time to wander about or we'll be late.

Here's a man selling all kinds of vegetables.

At school

It's 7.30 a.m. and we're just in time for school.
We do Hindi, English, Science, Geography, History,
Maths and Art as well as Sport and Music.
I really like Gym. School finishes at lunchtime.

This is me, in Hindi class. Hindi is one
of the languages we speak in India.

Here I'm ready for Gym.

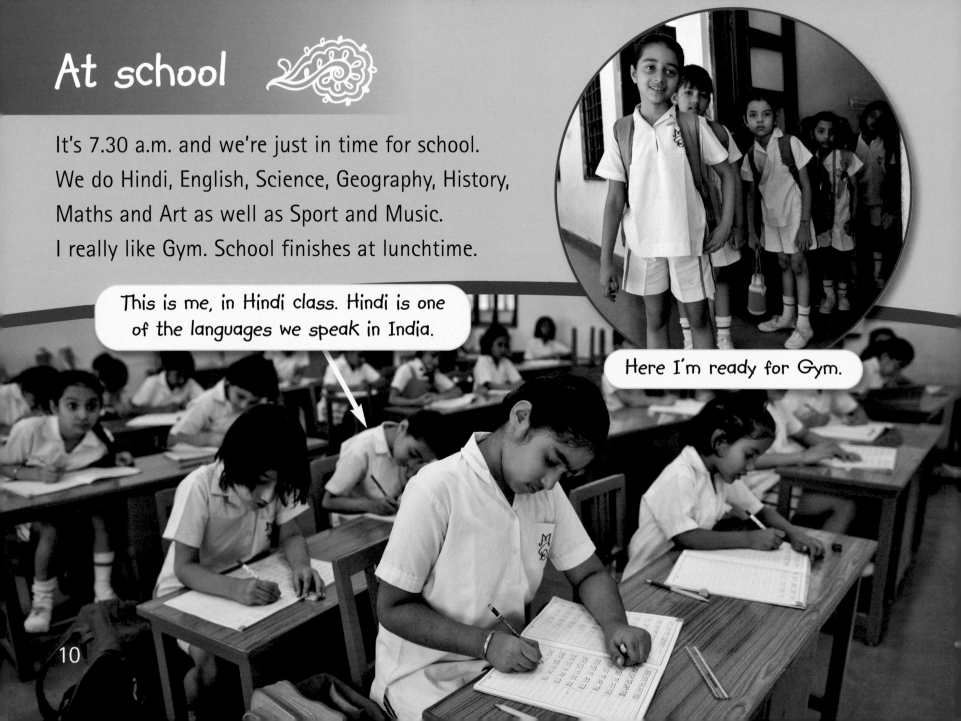

buying food at the snack shop

At break time we can buy snacks. I love lassi –
it's a drink made of yoghurt and sugar and
it's delicious, especially when the weather's hot.

This is my favourite:
lassi with mango.

11

Home time

At home time Mum and Dad come to pick me up in the car. Nila's school is further away, so she and her brother go home by bus.

the school bus

Nila and her brother are waiting for the school bus.

Nila's brother always wants to hang around in case his friends turn up to play cricket. Lots of Indian boys like cricket.

In the city, the roads are always busy and it can take us a long time to get home. We always see lots of tuk-tuks. They are small, three-wheel taxis without doors, and they whizz about in the traffic.

a tuk-tuk

A busy road in Jaipur: everyone is on the street, even the cows.

Sometimes you see a cow in the road with all the cars and buses and bicycles. No one wants to kill a cow, because they are special animals, so cows often wander where they like.

After school

As soon as we're home, Nila and I get changed and take our bikes out and play. We like to pretend that we're going on a long trip to find wild animals like tigers and crocodiles. Now we have the whole afternoon to play.

There really *are* wild animals in our garden. There's a monkey with her baby, a squirrel, and even a peacock.

some of the animals in our garden

Supper time

Before long, Mum calls us indoors to do our homework and then it's 7 p.m. and time for supper. It's fun when everyone talks about what's been happening that day. Tonight we've got my favourites – cottage cheese and salad and okra, which is a kind of vegetable.

cottage cheese

salad

okra

Bedtime

After supper, Raj goes to bed. It's nice and cool in the evening and Nila and I don't usually feel tired. We share a room, so we sit up chatting together. But we have to be up early the next day and by 9.30 p.m. we are fast asleep.

Once Raj is asleep, Mum often comes and talks to us.

Index

Things I like about where I live

the market

the clothes shop

Jaipur

my family

my school

Things I like about where I live

gym

22

my cousin Nila ——— playing in the garden ——— animals in the garden

lassi

food

supper time ——————— cottage cheese and salad and okra

23

Ideas for guided reading

Learning objectives: know how to tackle unfamiliar words that are not completely decodable; draw together ideas and information from across a whole text, using simple signposts in the text; explain organisational features of texts, including alphabetical order, layout, diagrams, captions; explain their reactions to texts, commenting on important aspects

Curriculum links: Geography: Passport to the world; Citizenship: Living in a diverse world

Interest words: Jaipur, yoghurt, Hindi, lassi, mango, okra, cricket, tuk-tuks

Word count: 676

Resources: world map or globe, whiteboard, ICT

Getting started

- Look at the front and back covers of the book and read the title and blurb together.

- Model how to read the word *Jaipur*. Ask children to recount strategies for tackling new words. Explain that place names might not be pronounced as children expect.

- Show children India on a globe or a world map. Ask children to share what they know about India. Record their ideas on a whiteboard. Prompt with questions if necessary, e.g. *What is the weather like there?*

- Read the contents page together. Ask children to predict what might happen in each stage of Gini's day.

Reading and responding

- Ask children to look at the contents page and read the section that interests them most, asking children to feed back the main points of their section to the rest of the group.

- Ask children to return to the contents page and choose another section to read, noting the non-fiction text features.

- Make a list of the non-fiction text features that children have found useful in their reading.

- Ask children to read through the whole book using using the non-fiction text features, e.g. photos and labels, to help them make meaning.